LIGHTKEEPERS

Also by Elizabeth Burns

COLLECTIONS

Ophelia and other poems (Polygon, 1991)
The Gift of Light (diehard, 2000)
The Lantern Bearers (Shoestring Press, 2007)
Held (Polygon, 2010)

PAMPHLETS

The Time of Gold (Galdragon Press, 2000)
The Alteration (Galdragon Press, 2003)
The Blue Flower (Galdragon Press, 2005)
The Shortest Days (Galdragon Press, 2008)
A Scarlet Thread (Wayleave, 2014)
Clay (Wayleave, 2015)
Plum (Wayleave, 2016)

LIGHTKEEPERS

Elizabeth Burns

Edited by Gerrie Fellows and Jane Routh

First published in 2016
by Wayleave
8 Buoymasters
St George's Quay
Lancaster LA1 1HL

www.wayleavepress.co.uk

ISBN 978-0-9935103-3-5

British Library Cataloguing-in-Publication Data
A catalogue record for this book is available from the British Library.

Cover image: 'Distance and Proximity' by Jane Rushton

Design and Typesetting by Gerry Cambridge

Printed by Glasgow Print + Design Centre
197 Bath Street, Glasgow G2 4HU
www.GlasgowPDC.co.uk

Contents

for Amy and Kezia

The recovery room

is where they wheel you afterwards; a kind of limbo
—place between earth and heaven where the body lies
before ascending—where you drift from sleep to waking.

There's a quiet, end-of-the-day feel, the nurses talking softly.
One brings you water, another helps you to your feet
and asks you how you like your tea. You put on slowly

your own clothes, totter over to the sofa,
the table set with magazines, a tin of biscuits. And this
seems all you'd ever need: the peaceful room,

the plate of processed cheese and crackers,
a few words with another patient, a glance
at the *National Geographic*, your tea replenished.

But someone says, *Your husband's here*, and he's standing
in the open doorway, wearing the clothes of the outer world,
his hat and scarf and coat on this November evening

and you are borne away on his arm, along corridors,
lightheaded with sedation and relief—the tests are clear—
ascending into cold fresh air, the winter on your skin.

The lilies

How you came on the bright afternoon of wind and sun
with your arms full of lilies and a box of eggs,
and we sat in the garden at the table with the cloth
made by our great aunt, and drank tea, ate scones,
and talked of how an object becomes sacred; as does
a space, made special by the laying out of cloth and flowers;
of how a nest placed in a woman's hands can heal her;
how new songs are being made for births and deaths
and celebrations; how metal from the spindle of a loom
in a cotton mill can be hammered flat, transformed
into the circles of a necklace. You're here for an hour,
and our lives are suddenly fresh, alive to possibility,
opening up like the petals of the lilies overnight.

Listening to Bach's B Minor Mass in the kitchen

Finally, I'm done with the phone calls and everything else
and when I switch on the radio it feels like lying in salt water—
all I need to do is breathe: Bach will keep me afloat.
I'm mixing yeast into flour, making rolls for my daughter's
birthday breakfast in the morning, kneading and kneading
the dough then setting it to rise; arranging in a glass
the last of the tiny pink roses with a sprig of green,
finding the blue candles and ironing the tablecloth,
the one my granny embroidered, sweeping the floor,
thinking about the hot August night of the birth,
and about the people we met on Westray last week,
and the presents I still need to wrap, and Bach himself
who is like a mountain covered in wildflowers,
and the singers in the Albert Hall who, the conductor says,
get *close to godliness* through this performance;
and I'm wondering, as all those voices fill my kitchen
with the Mass, if this is what he means: the sense
of time and place dissolving, so what divides us
from the past and elsewhere, and from each other,
falls away, and everything's connected and we are all
drops of water in this enormous breaking wave.

Making mendi

Sometimes it seems like a dream you were here in our home,
bright in our lives, my extra daughter for a fortnight, arriving
with bel poori and pearls, your sari, bangles, spicy noodles.

But like someone in a fairytale who wakes to find the object
they were given in a dream, I need only look down at my hand
where you made mendi on our last afternoon; your clear eyes

focussed on the needle-fine line of paste you squeezed
from the tube as if it were icing and my hand the cake,
tickled and marked with delicate drawings: a sacred drum

and its drumsticks, flowers on the backs of my fingers,
and in curly letters over the top of my palm, my name.
When it dried, I brushed off the paste, and there were the lines

on my skin, dark brown, indelible. My hand felt different;
I was careful of it, and aware, as if it had a healing wound,
a thing I must be gentle with and not get wet. After you'd left,

I kept glancing at it, and each time, a flicker of memory—
the boat across the lake, the picnic and the sunny garden,
playing card games, eating bowls of maggi by the open fire.

Curled in my fist like a secret, the mendi reminds me of you:
I know its pattern intimately now, so even when it fades
I'll remember this proof of your presence, its print on my skin.

The spool

By the late evening light from the window, I unpick
ten utilitarian buttons from my daughter's vintage dress
then, heads bent together, we sew on the new pearly ones
whose sheen picks up the pale pinks, mauves, greens
of the embroidered flowers. Five buttons each: she works
downwards from the neckline, I work up from the hem, saying
remember to wind the thread round the back of the button,
and thinking of all those generations teaching daughters
how to sew on buttons, of the tiny buttonhole stitches
of grandmothers and great aunts; and just as the light's fading
and we need the lamp, just as the thread from the old wooden reel
runs out, we meet in the middle, and the dress is ready for tomorrow
when she'll wear it with the lacy sea-green cardigan, her pearl earrings.
And here she is, early in the hot June morning, light on her feet
in her pretty shoes, setting off with her camera, her sketchbook,
on the school trip to the gallery, the art college show; threading her way
down the street, heading out into the promise of this summer's day.

Little Women

I'm lying in bed with this book my mother's given me,
a battered old edition, blue hardback, the title in gold,
the one she read as a girl (the one that, in forty years or so,
my own daughter will be reading). *Little Women:
A Story for Girls* says the title page, mottled with age.

My mother comes to say goodnight, turn off the light.
I'll carry on reading by torchlight, under the covers.
Perhaps we talk about the story—I don't remember now, only
that I turn to the inside cover, where there's a label,
signed on a Christmas day sixty years back
by a Sunday school superintendant. 'Presented to,' it says.

'Who was Winnie Hale?' I ask, not really expecting she'll know.
'She was my mother,' she says, 'my real mother.'
She tells me our Gran is her stepmother; that her real mother
died when she was eight. My motherless mother,
looked after by aunts, almost adopted (though this story
won't be told for years) by friends of the family.

Nothing remains of this grandmother, not even photographs.
Nothing of the poetry she wrote, that was found among her things.
Only *Little Women*: a book that I came to inhabit
reading it over and over again. A child lost in books,
in the drama of mother and daughters, and beginning to know

that what you love most can disappear, leaving only a trace:
my grandmother's name, written on that shiny label, red and gold,
inside her treasured book, and spoken at last by my mother
who once was forbidden ever to mention it. How not to sentimentalise
all this? Sad family story told through that most sentimental book.

By mentioning that I then made little figures—dolls, about four inches tall—
out of scraps of cloth and lace, with woollen hair, embroidered eyes
and called them Meg, Jo, Beth, Amy. Enacted scenes with them?
I can't remember. Only that they gave me comfort, and defiance—
if l had to play with dolls, they'd be dolls out of books, if l had to sew,
I'd make characters from stories. And they showed that books

had life beyond themselves, that things imagined could be real
and touchable as bits of felt and velvet. A prototype of writing,
using someone else's characters before I made my own.
Because of course the thing that *Little Women* showed you
was not just that people died but that even girls could write,
publish, see a story handed on; your name on the cover of a book.

The volumes

I get right inside the dictionary: my lovely two-volume Shorter Oxford.
—Gillian Allnutt

And all through the long months, this dark time
when she can scarcely leave the house, the girl
sits on her bed with her dictionaries beside her:
one volume open either side of her, their big pages
flapping like the wings of birds. Split down the middle
of the alphabet: Volume I, A-M, Volume II, N-Z.
Sometimes she prefers one, sometimes the other.
They are all she needs. When she's asked what she'd take
from a burning house, she says, *My dictionaries.*
The insides of words—their sounds and meanings,
their derivations, their complicated histories,
their fizzy mix of languages: Greek and Latin,
Anglo Saxon and Old Norse, French, German,
Middle English. So many stories here, a place
where the girl, so quiet, so solitary, can dwell for now,
until she is ready; ready to leave, and then
the fine onion-skin pages of her dictionaries
will turn to wings and she, like the boy in the fairytale
whose bones were buried under a juniper tree,
will become a bird, and take flight, and sing;
and when she comes back home, she'll turn,
as did the boy, from bird into human again,
not flightless now with wings laid flat on the bed,
but coming and going, carrying the weight of both
those lovely volumes with her, not a burden, but a gift.

The eggs

You do not need to know why or who or where from,
only that there were ten dozen duck eggs on our doorstep.
They are layered in trays made of soft blue cardboard,
the colour of sugar paper. I place the heavy, fragile tiers
on the floor, then the table, move them from room to room
so the eggs are haloed with morning or evening light,

cast their shadows onto one another. They become
a presence in the house. I love their magnitude,
their plenty, the rows and rows of them,
the different ways of ordering and counting them.
Their ranks of sameness, and their slight differences.
I run the back of my hand over their smooth cold nubs

or hold them in my palm, as if this is what it was made for.
Eventually I start giving them away. I give half a dozen
to the neighbour's boy who bakes us cookies in return,
I give some to a man I vaguely know wheeling his bike up the hill,
I give some to the woman who comes to borrow the car,
to the person whose mother knows where they came from.

We begin to eat them: I make a duck egg omelette,
a lemon cake with duck eggs, we boil and poach
and scramble them. Now there are only four left.
I don't want to use them, I want to keep them
on this windowsill and gaze at them each day—
their lovely shapes, the ovals clear and pure,

as if they were holy, made for ritual; the way
their shells in places are pinkish, like the blush
on white roses, which must come from the yolks

because blown, they're an almost bluish white;
and the way they are contained and unassuming,
holding inside themselves a freight of possibility.

Breakfast at Wuthering Heights

They knew about terrible porridge, the Brontës. They learnt it at school
where the porridge was burnt, the milk sour. In *Jane Eyre*, at Lowood,
it's *a nauseous mess* that no one can swallow. *Abominable stuff.*
When Heathcliff's wife comes to the Heights, the porridge she makes
is lumpy and cold. She throws her bowlful down; the dog devours it.
Years later, her son stirs his with *aversion*, refuses to eat.

But look what love can do with ordinary substance. Cathy and Hareton
have been out before breakfast, digging a flowerbed, planning a garden.
They're in trouble with Heathcliff—for laughing, for rooting up plants—
but they know he can't touch them: together, they're stronger than him.
Before Cathy was born, her father placed on his sick wife's pillow
a handful of golden crocuses, the first flowers emerging from snow.

When she died, the weather changed: primroses and crocuses
were hidden under wintry drifts, as if love too were buried and dead.
But this spring, at last, something's new: what has been under earth
is coming alive. What Cathy does echoes the gesture her father made—
a gift of yellow flowers for the beloved. She does it lightly and playfully,
making Hareton's breakfast into something beautiful, *sticking primroses*

in his plate of porridge. And here, on an April morning not long afterwards,
when Heathcliff's close to death and won't come down to breakfast,
Cathy and Hareton are eating theirs outdoors, a little table set for them
under the trees. They're escaping at last from the gloom of the house
and the weight of their past. They wrote about terrible things, the Brontës,
but look how their stories transmute them, lace them with honey and cream.

Marthe answers the *Guardian* art critic

'She mopes, she feeds the dog, but most of all Bonnard's missus washes herself...
Bathing and moping, indeed, seem to be what she does best.'

You think I bathe too much. I tell you
that water is where I belong, water

soothes and cleanses me. I wash and wash.
The bathroom's the place I inhabit

and he paints me there: he is in love
with the wet light on my skin, the curve

of my body, the ripple and fracture of water.
Yes, bathing is what I do best

and you cannot know what it is
to wash yourself over and over

and never feel clean. Pierre knows.
He brings his easel in: we are together

in that bathroom, it smells of turpentine
and lavender, of linseed oil and lemon soap.

I bathe, and he paints. This bath
is where I belong. And the moping?

Can you think how it feels
to have to turn your face away

and not be seen? I am not Renée
with her smiling open sunflower face—

I cannot pose for hours like that.
I look away, down, sideways, out of the picture,

not moping, only protecting myself
from the glare of your eyes.

Pierre understands: he will not paint my face
and trap it on the canvas for everyone to see.

It's as if l were made of worn old silk,
and turned towards the sunlight of too many gazes

I would disintegrate. I wash myself, I bow my head
down. These are the paintings he makes of me.

Dresser

The dresser has its own history, hidden in the wood
of its drawers and cupboard. The only parts I know

are these: that once it travelled across Europe,
over the channel and into a house in London

and then, years later, came to Clitheroe to be sold;
that one spring afternoon I too came to Clitheroe,

wandered into the antique shop, and saw there
a dresser, the one I'd searched for all these years,

a blue-painted dresser that was old and worn
and had six little drawers with knobs for handles,

a dresser that would fit exactly into my kitchen
—a finger's width between it and the ceiling—

a dresser that looks as if it belongs there,
stately and homely all at once. I unwrapped all the china

I'd been saving for this moment, and set it out—
the violet tea-set, the French coffee cup, the little dish

my grandmother bought on her honeymoon, the
rabbit toast-rack, the white porcelain bowl.

The dresser is scratched and some of its paint
is wearing away, but its wood glows in the evening sun

and it holds a bowl of oranges, perhaps, or a jug of roses,
green candles, blown eggs, tulips, herbs, postcards;

and if you take the key to the smooth brass keyhole
and unlock the cupboard, and open the little drawers

you'll find them filled with things like forks and drawing pins,
tablecloths and ginger beer and biscuit cutters

and in amongst all this, hidden inside the musty smells
with all the secret tales from long ago and far away,

new things are being added to a history, stories
that the blue and lovely dresser is keeping to itself.

The hours

after Burne-Jones 'The Hours'

Of course they're beautiful, this row of women
with their milk-white skin and soulful eyes,
their folds of drapery in gorgeous jewel colours;
but they're sleepy and vapid, as if with their distaffs and harps
they're here to represent the long bored hours
of Victorian women raised on tame accomplishments;
the sonorous, tedious hours of the drawing room,
the calling card, the polite and dull conversation.

You want to shake them from their pedestals,
put them onto bicycles that are about to be invented,
let them enter universities and hospitals, become
professors, surgeons, architects, astronomers;
let them be suffragettes, let them have the vote,
let their lives be packed with excitement and intellect
and vigour, the hands on the clock spinning round
so fast they don't know where the day has gone.

Hopkins in Preston

The church of St Ignatius on rainy afternoons
is a place of darkness: stained glass matt, unlit,
the only candleflame uncertain in the draft.
A gutter drips, stone slabs seep dampness.
Mixed with the incense, a factory stink in the air.

He is meant to be praying, he is meant to be
making intercession for the souls of the poor
of Preston: he must give himself over to this.
But here's the memory of the bluebell wood
not twenty miles away, so fresh after rain,
the way the drops glide down the crease
of a leaf, or cling to the tips of petals
so magnifying the centre of each flowerhead,
and the way the whole wood gleams and glistens
with the freshness of it, rinsed by spring rainfall,
the clean air full of the breath of bluebells—

It seems that everything in nature is whole, entire,
integral (the oak tree and the bluebell and the jackdaw
are simply themselves) yet he's split into poet and priest.
His brother an artist, his sister a nun: but he's riven,
cannot ever choose between these lives. Sometimes
it seems easier to snuff out the little flame of poetry.
During Lent he takes no meat, writes no verse,
tries to vanquish his unholy urge for fame.
Look, he is able to quell all that part of himself,
did so once for seven years, could do so again,
give up writing, devote his spirit completely
to the Jesuits.
          But still the words rush at him,

spill from him, fondle his mouth and his tongue,
the caressed, lovely sounds of the Mass,
and his own words, shaping themselves into lines
with their stresses, sprung rhythms. Yes, he can vow
not to write throughout Lent, but new-placed words
sing in his head like the first call of cuckoos in spring
and even unwritten, the stanzas will lodge in his brain
familiar as prayers, will come with his footfalls,
or break out in snatches, recited aloud.
His head's like a belltower, ropes pulled at random,
a jangle of voices. To achieve that clarity
he longs for, the one pure, fused note—

which is there in the swoop of the fields,
the curved shape of elms against sky, their inscape, the thing
that he touches and senses. Bluebell leaf, raindrop:
in each one its essence. In moments like this
he knows it's his gift and his task to put what he feels
into words, to be what he's made for, mortal, immortal,
spirit and body pursed into one, the priest and the poet,
variety, oddity—this is his quiddity, made for him,
mixed in him, disciple and servant of God, of his flock,
and of language, his master, his thraldom.
Words given flesh in him, words that will straddle him,
binding him, melding him, making him wholly himself.

And now he must carry this feeling, this sense
of himself, cupping his hands round its candleflame,
that it may not be quenched, as he walks down the aisle
and out into the streets of Preston on a dark wet afternoon.

A revolution

Look, they are renaming everything: streets, towns,
saints' days, coins, anything that's tainted with the old regime.
This is a new republic, power is heady: they'll abolish

what they want, invent new names and maps and systems.
They dream of classical ideas, of a kind of marbled whiteness,
a country run like clockwork, everything swept clean.

Even time has a new template laid on top of all the muddle
of the old: months have three weeks now, each week's ten days;
days are ten hours long, and an hour's a hundred minutes.

They make new clocks—a hundred seconds to a minute—
but who can go against the patterns of the sun and moon?
The clocks last only eighteen months, and are abandoned.

The new-named months last longer, they'll survive a dozen years:
month of the grape harvest, months of frost and fog, of snow
and wind and rain, though the weather doesn't always fit—

spring might be late and cold, the months of germination,
flowering, summer heat, all gone awry. Dates are confusing,
years numbered now from the birth of the republic.

It can't be done, this rigid grid of numbers, pasted over
what's irregular and messy. The same way
that the giddy new republic tries to cover up the Terror:

trials and executions, conspiracies and spies, an endless
cleansing of state and church. Swoop of the guillotine. Nothing
can wash away the blood, nothing can alter human nature.

There comes the Emperor. The calendar reverts to what it was.
A vestige: metric weights and measures, how long a bolt of cloth can be,
the dip and tilt of little bits of polished brass, balanced on the scales.

Engraving the sky

Caelum (Nicholas de Lacaille, 1713–62)

He wants to map the southern sky, to see a different hemisphere,
discover how the universe appears from somewhere else.
He sets sail for the Cape of Good Hope, builds an observatory,
catalogues ten thousand stars, finds new constellations
jostling in the dark with all those others named for creatures
or mythical beasts—*centaur, hydra, phoenix*, a footless bird.

He sees the shapes of his discoveries as echoes of inventions
he admires and names them *the microscope, the telescope,
the octant, the clock, the air pump, the mariner's compass*
and this one, almost the smallest of all he calls *the sculptor's chisel,*
though perhaps the name's too heavy, too unwieldy,
for this faint constellation that he draws as two engraver's tools—

one an etching needle, the other with a sharp tip, diamond-shaped,
the two crossed over, tied with ribbon, a ribbon that flows into space,
and where it ends, he marks the final star. Look at his crowded map
of the sky, see a dove with an olive branch, its wingtip
just brushing the shaft of the engraver's tool. Feathers and ribbon,
these soft things set against his endless calculations,

his tables of eclipses, of the moon's position, his mind whirring
with it all, running ahead of itself, out into space, into all those nebulae
that he was the first in the world to observe. And here he stands
in the warmth of an African night, gazing upwards; the sky,
he thinks, remembering his Lucretius, like a cup of darkness
held above us, a vessel engraved all over with stars.

How music travels

How ordinary this is and how peculiar:
that in a car on a motorway in England
at the end of the first day of the year
I am listening to people in Japan
singing music that was first sung
in Germany on a new year's day
almost three hundred years ago.
How ordinary because all I need to do
is touch a button and this music
fills the car: and how peculiar,
how miraculous, that singing
in Japan is trapped inside a silvery disc
and someone in London sets it free
and it travels through the winter air
and is inside this moving car.
And here are other miracles:
that a tune can be written down
in lines and circles, as this one was;
that the paper with these marks on
was not lost; that people can look at it
and bring the music back to life;
that although it was written
for one particular new year's day,
this cantata flew around the world
and into a future that no one
singing in an icy church in Leipzig
on the first day of 1724
could begin to imagine;
and that somehow it can lodge itself
inside the singers and the players
and the listeners and be carried
with them wherever they go —

In the house of Arnolfini

This house, like the streets and canals,
is made of straight lines—brickwork,

shutters, floorboards, windowpanes—
but something lurks in curves of mirrors,

is buried under furs and folds of garments.
He looks out from under the brim of his hat

knowing that nothing in his life before
has been as unpredictable as this.

It came to him suddenly during her pregnancy
that he must get Van Eyck the painter in

to make a portrait of his wife. It's as if she must
cross a river, green and flowing as her gown,

something vast and treacherous, and may perish
on the way. But nothing has ever been beyond him:

he will pay the best doctors in town, he will hire
extra women to help, every fire in house will be lit,

there'll be gallons of water brought from the pump,
and piles of folded linen for her bed.

He is standing still for the portrait,
watching the way she clutches at her dress.

His wife's hand in his, the blood in her veins,
the love in his heart. But they say that she's delicate:

look at her fingers, fine as spiders' webs,
and the whiteness of her skin as pale as milk—

Annunciation

after Hammershoi

Because it could have happened anywhere,
why not here, in the cold light of a northern winter,
the quiet interior of a house in Copenhagen,
the twentieth century not yet begun? Here,
among polished tables, tight-sheeted beds,
the gleaming black of the great iron stove
that she sweeps out every morning; here,
where in the afternoons, she pours coffee
into delicate cups for the mistress and her guests,
and later sweeps up crumbs, smoothes creases
from the tablecloth, tidies sheet music.

It's when she's in the kitchen making bread,
walloping the great mound of dough
at the scrubbed board table, that she senses
something close to her. At first she thinks
it's just a finger of sunlight touching her neck.
Then she remembers being a child, an old sheet
draped round her shoulders, believing she could fly.
And now it's as if she were lifted, her hands letting go
of the bread, and opening out. The precious house
falling away, so it's she who is fragile and cupped,
who is, for a moment, held. Her weightlessness

among the silver knives and copper pots;
this presence in the room she cannot touch.
The word angel is what comes to her,
but not like the ones in paintings, more as if she—
it sounds odd to say it—were becoming one;

that sense on her back of wings, making her
lightsome as she folds the loaves into their tins,
glazes them with milk and sets them by the stove
to rise. A slab of butter in a dish, pale yellow
like the winter sun. The bell rings, and she goes,
radiant, to her mistress, who would never believe—

The Visitation

after Stanley Spencer

She is used to miracle—she is a milkmaid, after all,
knows the daily gift of thin white liquid can be turned
to curds or cream, or churned to pats of yellow butter.
So when the dank, sour dairy was filled that day with light,
and an angel stood before her, she knew herself
transformed, felt in her body the tiny flame of a child
which she must tend. But who will believe her?

She'll get the sack for being pregnant, the village gossips
will whisper, and if she tells the truth, they'll say
she's mad, pack her off to the asylum. Where can she go
but here? Who else can she tell but her cousin?
She, the butcher's daughter, who is used to the spill of blood
mopped up by sawdust, the slice of a knife through flesh,
and who knows for herself the wonder of conception.

And knows by now the bloom of pregnancy, can sense it
in her little cousin, who has turned up out of the blue,
urgent, anxious, yet with a quiet radiance about her
as she stands there framed by corrugated iron roofs
and new green leaves, her pinafore white as sails,
the frills around its shoulders looking like little wings.
Their sturdy hands are clasped: they are two women

linked by kinship, by news brimming over like milk
from an overfull pail. The older woman, like a tree
in her greens and browns, draws the young girl
over the threshold, says she must sit by the fire,

they'll have tea and hot crumpets, and she will listen.
So Mary, fresh in her blue and white as the April sky,
comes inside, begins to tell her everything.

Emmaus

after Velasquez 'Kitchen maid with the Supper at Emmaus'

She's taken them out some bread, a jug of wine,
and thought that she—dark-skinned kitchen maid—
would pass among them invisibly as breath.

But he, the stranger they'd met on the road,
looked her straight in the eye, thanked her
for the food and drink; saw who she was.

Back in the kitchen among bowls and jugs,
pestle and mortar, cloves of garlic, she's distracted,
stands with her back to the hatch, trying to hear

what's happening in the other room.
She's listened all weekend to rumours of death
but now, this evening, in this inn,

a man is breaking the bread she gave him,
and his companions, amazed, are speaking his name—
She fingers the edge of the kitchen table,

the curve of a jug she'll fill with more wine,
bring over to them with some fish, a bowl of olives
that she'll set beside the stranger,

letting him see that she too knows who he is:
that she is witness to a resurrection,
has seen him risen, as he's seen her.

Cupboard

In the dark ages, an acorn took root and grew into an oak
they said was sacred. Then Oswald came and turned its wood
into an altar. A church grew, saplings from the old oak grew,
and perhaps this church's heavy door was made from one of them.
Hundreds of years of wind and rain: wood split and warped.
They took the door down, and from its remnants, fashioned
a cupboard. A century later, and a woman nearly as old
as the cupboard itself is still caring for it, remembering days
with her grandmother as she polishes the hinges and the row of hooks,
rubs the keys that hang there to a gleam, feeds the cracked old wood
with beeswax. Her mind turns somersaults thinking about the door
of the church becoming the door of the cupboard, a little replica,
with lock and hinges, and how a key can open up a cupboard
holding keys to other cupboards. Everything is inside everything else,
the way her grandmother is inside her (the shape of her nose,
her fingernails, how they are both content in the quiet of the church)
and inside her grandmother is another grandmother and so on,
back to people who opened the oak door when it was new
under its lintel, and further back to Oswald and the altar,
to ancestors who worshipped the oak tree, which came from the acorn.

The balance

As if, in the convent kitchen, these things
were balanced in the old brass scalepan:
shrivelled lemon and chalky-white stone

Our austerity, the thing that sometimes
sours and wizens us, makes us hard as stone,
bitter with regret, and longing for

the lemon tree in the whitewashed courtyard,
its green fruit ripening in the sun,
the taste of honey in our mouths—

But then the good, clean hardness of the stone
worn smooth, its pure shape like the pieces
of evening light slanting on the walls

like an egg, warm in my palm, like our voices
threaded together, singing and rising,
the round hollow of the soul, filled.

Austerity

suited my father, back in the fifties when he was lean and spare,
living in the tiny house at the plain address, 1 Back Lane,
with a packing case for a table where he pours tea for his friends
who live in a caravan and have come round for a bath—
He and Mum eat bashed tins of veg from the canning factory.
He has no car, he cycles everywhere, and when I am born
and it's a Sunday with no buses, he hitches to the hospital.
When my mother brings me home at last, it's Christmas Eve
and because there's no money for a tree, he's made one
out of plywood with his fretsaw, a cut-out he props up
on the wedding-present sideboard. Look how the standard lamp
casts its soft glow over the wooden tree, the bowl of fruit
and vase of daffodils given in celebration of my birth (fresh grapes
and flowers in winter!). Even my father's eyes if we could see them
would be shining, for he is fuelled by love for his new bride,
his baby daughter. My father at this moment in his life
owns very little, yet if you'd asked him if there was anything
he needed, he'd grin and say he lacked for nothing.

The hare

No one knows his name, or anything about him
except he must have been a master craftsman

cutting little chunks from sticks of limestone,
sandstone, brick or marble—his palette of colours—

and placing the chosen tesserae so carefully,
making this floor-pattern of intricate knotwork

surrounding a circle, and here at the centre,
the hare. No one remembers his name, but look

how he makes an animal come alive—
look how he's shaded the colours of fur,

its soft greys and browns, laid tiny cubes of glass
to give glints of light to the curve of the back;

look at the grey-blue circle of the eye, the pink
inside the ears, look at the nibbling mouth,

eating a succulent plant, think of the quiver
of nose, sniffing it; look at the scut and the taut,

muscular haunches, the back legs ready to spring,
to leap up from this floor and out into grass,

speeding through fields, over hills, bounding
through spring, season of madness and delight—

His name's forgotten, but look what he made us
nearly two thousand years ago—his gift

from the past to the future, picture of a creature
cut from stone: this living, breathing hare.

Lightkeepers

There was nothing to mar your days, if you were a boy summering in that part,
but the embarrassment of pleasure.
—Robert Louis Stevenson

Not destined to build lighthouses, as his father's family do—
but look how he writes about darkness and light, the bucket
the child sees at night time, *half full of water and stars*;
the lamplighter coming at dusk to illuminate the street.

He is born to this story: the way light in darkness
can save us, and each childhood summer is spent on the coast,
close by the blink of the Isle of May lighthouse, the Bass,
making up stories of pirates and shipwrecks, climbing Black Rock

as my children do, year after year, the house where we stay
three doors along from the Stevensons' villa, so I see Louis
head for the rockpools, climb the hill at the back of the houses
or go that way to the cliffpath—his friendly ghost is everywhere.

He's with us on the boat trip to the Bass Rock, the place
he imprisons his hero. On our way back to land, a haar
breathes suddenly over the sea, swallows the cliffs and the islands,
the harbour, the town. Another boat looms, like something from a dream,

shapes appear out of whiteness then vanish, like flashes of memory—
our days on this beach, those moments of delight I want to pull clear
of their shadows: our stay here never long enough, the summers
of my daughters' childhoods slipping through my hands like sand.

Back on land, hot sun eases through fog, the girls shake off
their teenage selves—all week they've been combing their wind-tangled hair,

drinking cappuccinos, looking in shops—and build sandcastles
with moats, potter in rockpools like they used to. Our last evening

and I walk until the Fidra lighthouse starts flickering across the sea.
Wet sand holds the sunset, makes it liquid, and I want to store all this
—landscape, happiness—inside me, preserve it. But it's fragile as glass,
a lantern-slide lit for a moment, then laid over others and blurred.

I walk along the links, as Stevenson did in the late summer dusks,
meeting other boys at a hollow in the sand where they'd show
the little tin lanterns they'd bought and tied to their belts,
not to shine out like lights hung from fishing boats, not visible

like the ones policemen wore: the thing was to hide the light
under your coat, only show it when you met another boy.
Stevenson looks back and sees it as an image of the gleam
that makes us human, the fiery, unquenchable self we all carry

under the guise of our bodies. We're lightkeepers, making ready
for sundown, revealing that tiny glimmer and refracting it.
We walk back together, he and I, down past the harbour, along
the East beach, the last of the sunset behind us, Black Rock ahead,

our lanterns glowing in the secret dark. The lightbeams
from the islands flare across the sea, beacons in darkness.
We come to the end of the road. His is the last house.
We take what light we can to keep us through the night.

Equinox

Here is the start of the year: Lady's Day,
birth of spring, daylight outgrowing the dark.
Out in the Galloway hills, the twilit blue sky
holds a full orange moon, and the farewell fire
at the edge of the woods is still small enough
to vault, like the fires lit in spring in the streets
of Iran, where pain and sickness turn to ash
as you leap, taking life from the breath of the flames.

This bonfire's enormous now, windblown and orange,
fiercely hot in the cold Scottish night, sparks flying up,
flecks of light in the dark, like the snowdrops
marking the path that leads to the house,
their whiteness lit up by the globe of the moon
that's risen now, yellow and round as a sun.

Sea-loch

High tide this week is early morning, so you wake
to a full still loch glassily holding the greens of the hillside.

Northwards, its placid surface is pale mirrored cloud
and white reflections of houses scattered on the other shore

then ripples come, a quivering of waves, slight as a shrug,
as the sea starts pulling all five miles of water back

towards itself, dragging the loch away from the land
till it shrinks and a shoreline appears: bladderwrack,

crabshells, mackerel creels, beached rowing boats,
grass for the sheep. Now you can walk easily across

dark rock and yellow seaweed, over the gravelly floor,
all the workings of inlets exposed, an underside revealed

then covered over—a slow seeping, now bigger folds of water,
the push of tide heaving waves into this narrow space,

shoving seawater in so quickly it looks like a river in spate,
rushing towards the head of the loch, where it stops,

becomes shallower, eases into fields of bog myrtle
and meadowsweet. Quiet now, with little lapping waves

like breaths of the far-off tide, this great lung
of sea-loch rising and falling all day long.

Hest

This odd landscape at the edge of the bay: a maze of ditches and channels and pools, cutting through mud and sand and grass. Not like a proper beach—at high tide there's no gradual shallowness, or shelving of the sea, just a sudden sharp drop like a riverbank where muddy water slops up against it.

slippy-edged ditches
nowhere to land
if you jump

You start out next to the white-painted signal box, walk over the level crossing, or else the metal footbridge, high above the tracks from where you can see the sweep of the beach, the layers of the fells.

the old station closed now
trains rush through
just glimpsing the sea

This is the place where shells heap up, white cockles sprinkled over grass, crackling underfoot. The pile shifts slightly with the tides, is never in quite the same place. And this is where a midden must have been, because the mud hoards scraps of old china: half-buried slivers of plates and cups, a jug handle, the bottom of a bottle, bits of willow pattern.

among cockleshells
broken crockery—
two kinds of vessels

Sometimes the land's so wet it seems to be water-meadow, full of floating sky.

after the high tide
the flattened grass, the sodden
resilient plants

In winter, the pools and channels may be lidded with ice—touch
the lip of their frozen flaps, and they will tilt and dip, the water
underneath them quivering.

silver light on waterweed—
each pool-edge
rimmed with tinsel

Up above the beach, a short stretch of cliff-path, lined with wind-
bent hawthorns. From this high field you can see the whole bay,
its promise of a wide beach which, if you try to walk on it, will be
mudflats, sinking sands, dangerous river channels.

what look like rocks
are made of compacted mud
sometimes they crumble

Once they unloaded coal from here onto barges: canal, road,
railway, sea, all running parallel. Now the shoreline's in a different
place, and the old jetty sits out at sea, sunk in the mud, spikes of
wood sticking out with rusty bolts and barnacles stuck to them. At
low tide you can walk to it and stand there, facing out to sea, as if
you were on the prow of a ship.

oystercatchers
nibble at mud, then the whole flock
lifts into air

When the tide's far out, it seems there is nothing but crinkled
mud—hollowed and shadowed, rippled and dappled. On a winter
afternoon of low sun, it gleams with gold.

tides ease in and out
there are hardly ever waves
this is all flat water

You head back across the tracks, knowing that in your absence,
the shoreline will be altered. The bay moves and sinks and rises,
is never settled, never still. The pools and channels and ditches
empty and fill, the mud bubbles and oozes and shivers.

from the bridge, a last glance—
lines of sea, hills, sky
and a rising moon

Midsummer sundial

Your body's the marker—put your feet on the date
and the line of your shadow will lie on the hour,
somewhere between three and four o'clock,
a stripe of light travelling, falling through you,

telling the time. Everywhere you look
are verticals that could be sundials
with a circle of hours drawn round them—
across the bay, wind turbines, the mountains;

closer up, pylons on the estuary, cooling towers,
highrise flats, leafy trees, the spire of the cathedral,
even these buttercup stalks around the sundial;
each thing laying down its map of shadow

on the earth, its record of where sunlight was
on the afternoon of the longest day, the widest day,
full of the sky and the bay, the warm breath of summer,
and so many hours of daylight still to come.

The field

This summer I've taken to leaving the park by the other gate,
the one further up the road, so I can walk past the part of the field
they've stopped mowing, letting the grasses and the wildflowers
grow so they sway and waver in the breeze; and sometimes
when the weather's dry and the ground isn't flooded and muddy,
I stand here on what once was moorland, looking at the view,
or walk among the buttercups and clover and the sorrel,
the pinks and whites and yellows of the new-made meadow
where grammar school boys from down the hill were brought
to see Catholics disembowelled, the hangings from the gallows.

Wildflower hunt

The hunt begins in the spring of your eightieth year
as the land thaws and plants start to quicken

The equinox, and that luscious rush of early summer
its flourish of green, and lit petals, light evenings

All through the long summer months, your keen eyes
are noticing, searching, and each new flower you spot

is a gift, an achievement, sometimes expected
sometimes a surprise—discoveries and rarities

You hunt on the shore, on dune slacks and marshland
in the city, the town, on pavements and walls

You hunt by the railway, the roadside, a churchyard,
roundabouts, carparks, landfill, canal bank

You hunt at quarries and bings, woodlands and wasteground,
by rubbish dumps and sewage works, a stagnant pond

There are wildflowers everywhere—here, amongst heather tufts,
by a puddle on a wet track, on a tangled grassy slope

And now as the year turns to winter—leaves fallen
flowers faded—and all that you've found is hidden again

the hunt is over, your treasure gathered in
Yet there's nothing to hold in your hands—

all of it's conjured, imagined, remembered
in your list of names and places, photographs, descriptions

The hunt is over, and this place you live in is richer
than you'd ever dreamed: such an abundance of wildflowers

The hunt is over and here's the treasure trove: your knowledge
flying out like windblown seeds, and taking root in all of us

who've watched you exploring and observing and recording
bearing witness to what's growing all around us.

Scots / grass

(*The Scots Thesaurus,* 1990)

blaw grass, suggeroun, cannach, flee
lachter, fushloch, windlestrae, tathe
ronnachs, lonnachs, quicken, rammock
string gairse, ket, bruckles, pry
risp, rash, bennel, sprat
gairdener's gairtens, siller shakers
aits, wite, bere, haver
brockit, bruckit, brashloch, masloch
uncorn, sleepies, kemps

Willow song

The willow barn is full of swallows

    By all-hallows they will have flown

And out in the flooded fields

    We'll walk the alleys between willows

Watching for swellings, blemishes, weevils

    Culling the silver wands: harvest of willows

Swallowtail   *Woolly Willow*   *Silverleaf*

    Laid in water, made pliable, mellow

Gosling catkins, sessiles, dipped in glycerine

    Violet willow   *Golden Willow*   *Golden Sally*

The making of swills and balls

    Weaving of willow's filaments

Black Sally   *Silky Willow*   *Almond Willow*

    And what remains is willow kindling

Its smell, its woodsmoke, pulled

    Into the air the way the swallows are

The Weave

The way the light falls, lays its shadow on the willow
or through the densest weave makes pinprick cracks

inside a dark interior; the way there are spaces in between
the bends of hazelwood or ling or ash, where the weave's

so loose, so delicate the sculptures are made half of air—
these openings and shifts of light are what makes the forms

an echo of our lives, where all that's tangible and solid
is interlaced with absence, silence, memory,

things that are invisible, and we are woven vessels
as airy as those made out of ash or hazel, willow, ling.

The plum tree at night

Spring

The bright flowers of its blossom
are all that's visible in the dark—
a circle, a shower of white against
the black sky, a tree made of light.

Summer

No one to see the fat plums
thudding to the ground
but in the morning, here they are—
the soft earth's purple harvest

Autumn

Windy nights—the tree bends
and sways, all its leaves
pulled loose. After the storm,
you wake to naked branches.

Winter

Snow overnight, softly falling,
laying itself along the branches,
covering over all the places
where buds will emerge.

Cinquain at Dove Cottage

small white
turnip, pulled up
earth on its roots, the same
earth as when Dorothy Wordsworth
dug it

Dorothy Wordsworth's Haiku

sitting a long time alone
in the slate quarry—
the crescent moon

November—
the brook in places
still shaded with leaves

small greyish clouds—
the bright stars
hiding themselves

gathering mosses
in the green lane—
too dark to see

white fields
dark yew tree
bowl-shaped moon

by the lakeside
waterfowl calling—
one large star

branches of broom
wave gently—
the weight of snow

a housetopfull of snow
falls on the path—
the sound echoes

the snow a cushion—
in its centre
a young foxglove

the lake still—
until the breezes
make it alive

two stars
like butterflies
look far nearer than the moon

a quiet night—
the fire flutters
the watch ticks

the rough lake—
a boat
floats by itself

crows—
shapes of water
passing over fields

island sheep
reflected in water
look like those deer

the cleaned-out well
full of water—
still muddy

sun lays silver
on the backs of sheep—
animals from another world

                              about nine o'clock—
                              the sorrel leaves
                              opening

the sky
bluer than usual
around the full moon

                              through closed shutters
                              the sounds of birds
                              singing

a sullen evening
but at the boathouse
sudden sunlight

                              swallows
                              singing low
                              like muffled robins

breathless grey day—
golden woods
quiet in their decaying

in the green moss
three primroses
rearing up

Three found poems from the life of Winifred Nicholson

All her life she painted flowers

Flowers wrapped in paper   Flowers in a glass

Flowers in moonlight   Flowers in the snow

Snowflakes and aconites   Snowdrops and bittersweet

Winter hyacinth   Star of Bethlehem

Narcissi in basket   Crocuses in bowl   Daffodils in pewter jug

Madonna lilies, ancient Corinth   Japanese anemones, Paris

Greek hill flowers   Vases from Brittany

Flowers from the copper mine   Striped jug of flowers

Bankshead flowers in alabaster vase

Helen's bunch in Helen's pot

Nursery bunch   Two nosegays   Pinks and roses

Summer flowers in a glass vase

Poppies   Iris   Honeysuckle and sweetpeas

Late summer flowers   Blue mountain flowers

Borage in a sunlit window

Flowers in a peat bog, Iona

Hebridean roses   Dusky cranesbill

Wildflower windowsill

Dresser with some belongings of Winifred Nicholson's

jug   Staite Murray pot   Jean Hugo picture   Bernard Leach pottery

shells   Egyptian alabaster   Lucie Rie pottery   goblet   Ben Nicholson box

bottle   Alfred Wallis ship   mug   Hans Coper pot

stone   Lucie Rie jug and cup   striped pottery   Ben Nicholson box

During World War II, she names the colours

mud   earth   dust   beige   dun   khaki

pea green   grass green   duck's egg green

lavender   larkspur   daffodil

knife blue   air force blue   steel

sugar pink   baby ribbon blue   forget-me-not

lead   slate   shadow   dragon's blood

tobacco   wine   black coffee   chocolate

ruby   lemon   hyacinth   apricot   coral

flame   fire   sky   midnight   pitch

'Islay'

after Jane Rushton

how a painting slowly resolves itself
into sky and sand and water
into breaking waves   reflections

how it is all of this   and none of this
is simply lines and squares
of sea-green   grey-green   blue-green

*

shape and colour
becoming landscape

landscape becoming
shape and colour

*

(a memory of Bowmore
pale sand   flat waves
softness of a September morning)

*

through rubbed paint
white emerges

ripples perhaps   or cloud
an under-layer of light

and the just-darker horizontal
a suggestion of land   of hills

*

a place where paint
is fractionally yellower

enough to imply   a sandbar
or sun or water

—to look at the painting

opens up a space
like the wide expanse of a bay

opens up a memory
of a day   a place

opens up the heart
to lightness

'Set adrift'

after Jane Rushton

It's she, this unknown Inuit woman,
who inhabits the painting, whose words,
seen faintly as if under ice, are visible,
invisible through lines of pale blue-greens,
shadowy cloud-shapes floating like ice floes,
and small squares of a cold, greenish sea-white:
colours of Greenland, beneath whose surface
language hovers, the ghost of her poem,
of her sea and river, wind and sky, the things
that *encompass* her, make her *tremble with joy.*

Hepworth Wakefield

Inside the gallery, density
of bronze, marble, burnished wood
and a huge white plaster shape:
through its oval spaces, a window
and the river's sheen as it smoothes itself
over the weir; then tumble and bubble
and rush, quiver of water and light,
wind-blown clouds.
                The sculptures
stand solidly over the river view,
their hollows containing, as well as air
and their own scooped-out places
of silence and completeness,
all the dash and flitter of water,
its velocity, fluidity, transparency.

Vase

after Grete Marks

How the shape of it, like two spheres
melded, one above the other, resembles
the roundness of a body; and how
you want to curve your palm over it,
feel the smooth clay, a sea-green glaze
brush-splashed with rust-red;
to finger that crescent moon handle,
or blow softly over the opening,
hearing the song of your breath
inside the hollows of the vase
whose walls contain invisible air
as the body holds the soul.

And then recall how Goebbels saw it:
queer-looking, foreign, made by a Jew.
Degenerate. Containing nothing.

Eighty years or so later, another potter
will take the ashes of a man he mourns
and fold them into the clay of a jar;
and looking at this perfect sea-green,
rust-red vase, you think of all the ashes
that it might contain: those of the burned
books, the burned paintings, those of the
people not seen as intricate vessels
containing their own particular selves,
but only as degenerate pots,
not to be held or lovingly touched,
but only to be smashed to bits.

Globe

In the beginning, universe was, and inside that,
galaxy was, and as many stars as grains of sand
and in amongst this, a planet with its mineral crust;
then humans came, began scooping up wet clay,
rounding it into the size and shape of cupped palms,
drying it under the sun. Then came wheels and kilns,
and it was found that ashes of a fire could turn to glaze,
and it seems no time at all until that moment
when you made this globe of a pot, dipped it
in the deep green glaze, and then the paler one
that crystallizes on the deep and shining surface,
making specks of white like a sprinkling of stars;
thicker and more grainy round the dark neck
of the pot where they're clustered like a galaxy.

Spiral

From the spin of the wheel
comes a spiral
threading itself
up through the vessel
until it reaches the rim

where this twist in the clay
slips into air
then travels on invisibly
beyond the turning earth
and up into the whirling stars.

Editors' Notes

Between the publication of *Held* in 2010 and her death in 2015, Elizabeth wrote an astonishing number of poems. She continued to write to those central themes she had pursued throughout the whole of her writing life—'women's ways of seeing and writing', giving voice to the 'unseen' and the 'silent, and making what was invisible, visible through words and images'. But she also wrote poems for friends and family, marking birthdays and anniversaries and events. She produced several pamphlets, one of which, *Clay* was shortlisted for the 2015 Ted Hughes Award and was runner up in the 2016 Callum Macdonald Award. She was commissioned to write poems of place for Lancaster Litfest and was involved in collaborative projects with a painter and a photographer in the Yorkshire Dales, and with a choreographer in another area of that same landscape. She worked with a painter and a potter on what became the 2015 Edinburgh Fringe exhibition 'Potter, Painter, Poet'.

When she asked us, shortly before she died, to put together this collection for her, she gave us no indication which of all this work we should include. But reading and re-reading her work we found we did have guidelines: poems that Elizabeth had published in magazines—or had sent out to an editor for consideration—were clearly pieces that she herself wanted to see out in the world. *Held* itself was another guideline: we could see how many good poems she hadn't included in that collection in order build a strong book and a flow through its pages. On the whole, Elizabeth didn't include personal poems addressed to family and friends in her collections so we too have followed this pattern. We also decided, with the exception of 'Spiral', against including poems from recent pamphlets which are in print and readily available elsewhere.

Interviewed for Lancashire Writing Hub in 2012, Elizabeth said 'I often write quite long, discursive poems, though I enjoy the opposite too—very short, condensed poems of just a few lines, and would like to be able to write more of those'. She did write more, many already published in her 2015 pamphlets *A Vessel Opening Out* and *Clay*. Because a reader brings different qualities of attention to the two different forms, in this collection which spans the full range of Elizabeth's writing, we have grouped these shorter poems together.

Is this the collection Elizabeth herself would have prepared? We are confident she would have included most of these poems in her next collection. But if ever we wondered whether a poem were quite finished, or felt a line didn't sound right, we didn't include it. We made no changes to the poems themselves: our editing has been a process of selection and ordering, not one of re-writing. So Elizabeth's collection would certainly have been a different one: every comma scrutinised, every page of hers polished and re-polished! That Elizabeth is no longer here to make these fine judgements is both a loss and a risk for us as fellow-poets and editors. We have understood our task as being not to memorialise (though for both of us she was a friend of longstanding), but to produce in her absence the nearest we could come to the collection she had not had time to complete.

We are grateful to Elizabeth's family for their help and enthusiasm while we prepared this collection.

—*Gerrie Fellows and Jane Routh*

Acknowledgements

Thanks are due to editors of the following publications where some of these poems first appeared:

Poetry Salzburg Review, Poetry Scotland, The Compass, The Dark Horse, The Scores; Heavenly Bodies ed R. Bilkau (Beautiful Dragons Press 2014), *Solstice* eds S. Hymas & R. Bilkau (Beautiful Dragons Press 2012), *Yesterday's Music Today*, ed R. Loydell and M. Ferguson (Knives Forks and Spoons Press 2015).

'Dorothy Wordsworth's Haiku' was originally produced as a limited edition of boxed cards by Essence Press in 2015. 'Spiral' accompanied the exhibition 'Potter, Painter, Poet' (Edinburgh Fringe Exhibition 2015) in *A Vessel Opening Out* and won a public vote for display on a giant banner on the Royal Mile over the winter of 2015/16; 'The Visitation' was commissioned for *The Hunterian Poems* ed Alan Riach (Freight Books 2015); 'Annunciation' won Manchester Cathedral Poet of the Year 2013; 'Listening to Bach's B Minor Mass in the Kitchen' won the BBC R3 Proms Poetry Competition 2012; 'Cupboard' was commissioned by St Oswald's Church, Grasmere, for the exhibition 'Holy Detritus' (2013); 'Wildflower hunt' is based on an earlier poem commissioned by Paul Tebble.

The editors have endeavoured to trace all previous publications of poems, but would be glad to know of any they have missed.